About t

I live in Fareham, Hampshire, with my wife Theresa and our 4 children. My own school reports have disappeared now, but I remember they were always brilliant.
Michael Coleman

Don't believe him. We found his reports hidden in the attic and they're awful. Our favourite was the one that said, 'Michael's conduct is satisfactory when he is under supervision, but he tends to behave rather foolishly at other times.'
Jennifer Coleman, Stephen Coleman, Catherine Coleman and Matthew Coleman

He hasn't changed.
Theresa Coleman

TUTANKHAMUN
IS A BIT OF A
MUMMY'S BOY

... and 50 other unpublished
school reports

MICHAEL COLEMAN

Illustrated by
Richard Duszczak

RED FOX

A Red Fox Book

Published by Random House Children's Books

20 Vauxhall Bridge Road, London SW1V 2SA

A division of Random House UK Ltd

London Melbourne Sydney Auckland
Johannesburg and agencies throughout the world

First published by Red Fox 1992
Reprinted 1992 (twice)

Text © Michael Coleman 1992

Illustrations © Richard Duszczak 1992

Printed and bound in Great Britain by
Cox & Wyman Ltd, Reading, Berkshire

ISBN 0 09 988180 2

To the pupils of
St. Judes' School, Fareham,
who *never* get reports like these
. . . well, hardly ever.

Contents

Introduction

Did you know that Dracula's teacher reported him for not being able to get up in the mornings? Or what Frankenstein's tap dancing teacher had to say about him?

Do you know why Tarzan's elephant was expelled from school but his chimpanzee wasn't? Or how Ben Hur got on when he tried to win his chariot-driving proficiency badge?

And did you know that Tutankhamun's teacher thought he was a bit of a Mummy's boy . . .

No, of course you didn't. Neither did anybody else – until now!

Years of painstaking research have discovered 51 school reports and letters to parents. Dracula, Ben Hur, Cinderella, Dr. Who, Julius Caesar . . . even ET . . . all proving that you're not the only pupil in history to have dreaded bringing home that long brown envelope.

THE
VAMP HIGHER SCHOOL
TRANSYLVANIA

Name of Pupil: DRACULA, COUNT

AGE: 13

Subject: Attendance and punctuality

Dracula's punctuality is appalling.
What is the matter with the boy,
can't he get up in the morning? To
look at him, you would think he had
been out all night.

I'm sure his health is suffering.
He must get up so late he can't
possibly have had time for a bite to
eat.

Yesterday he missed the annual
cricket match against our deadly
rivals, Frankenstein's Middle School
– a match we need not have lost had
it not been for his absence. It made
my blood boil, I can tell you. What
chance have you got without your
opening bat?

I really wonder whether Dracula's heart is in his school work. Does he not realise what is at stake? He makes me very cross. Unless he starts to put in a lot of effort he will end up without any qualifications at all; what a sucker he'll look then.

No, things must improve immediately. Every member of staff is fed up to the back teeth with Dracula's lateness. It used to be regarded as just a pain in the neck, but no longer. It's now a matter of grave concern.

I want to see him change! Overnight!

Brunhilde Sauerkraut

Brunhilde Sauerkraut
Form Mistress

DOUBLE DUTCH
SCHOOL

Name of Pupil: GOGH, Vincent Van
Age: 12
Subject: Music

Vincent has absolutely no ear for music. I suggest he takes up Art instead.

OBOE

Mrs O. Boe
Head of Music

STICKEMUP
GRABBER SCHOOL

Name of Pupil: TURPIN, Richard
Age: 13
Subject: Good Citizenship

Richard certainly has a long way to go if he
is to make progress in this subject.

Good Citizenship is about learning to live in
peace and harmony with your neighbour. It is
unfortunate, I grant you, that Richard's
complexion is less than perfect. Being called
'Spotted Dick' by one's neighbour does not
exactly encourage peace and harmony.

However, the fact that one is being called
names does not give one an excuse to act in
the appalling manner that we have seen from
Richard of late. He has become nothing less
than a highwayboy.

His method is quite simple. He searches for a
victim by galloping around the playground on
his trusty steed, Black Bess. The fact that
Bess is one of the stronger girls in school
and doesn't seem to mind spending her lunch
breaks dressed in a bin liner is neither here
nor there. Good Citizenship is about being

kind to one's neigh-bour, not frightening them
on a neigh-girl. Besides which, Richard's
spurs are making holes in Bess's cardigan.

Neither is it Good Citizenship to threaten
these victims with harm if they refuse to
hand over something of value. As I recently
pointed out to Richard, Good Citizenship is a
matter of give and take.

What was his reply? 'That must make me a Good
Citizen, Miss, 'cos I give 'em one in the eye
and then I take what I want!' Clearly the boy
has a long way to go before he's grasped the
essentials in this area.

After his experience this morning Mr
Bramwell, our Headmaster, will undoubtedly
agree with me. Accompanied by Mrs Bramwell,
he arrived at school only to be met at the
gates by Richard demanding: 'Stand and
deliver! Your money, or your wife!'

Really, this will not do. Richard must try a
lot harder to get the hang of this subject.
And Mr Bramwell wants Mrs Bramwell back by
the start of next term, please.

M. Bezzlement

M. Bezzlement
Form Mistress

ROME SCHOOL
FOR YOUNG OFFENDERS

Memorandum to: The Governor

Offender No. 281745

MICHAELANGELO (Buonarroti)

Offender 281745 (Michaelangelo) has buckled down well to life behind bars. Some of the credit must go to our warders, who are also very good at buckling - with the end of their belts, mostly - but 281745 has played his part.

Being put to work in the painting department has helped.

Given 281745's record, this was a bold and imaginative move by our Director of Forced Labour. After all, the boy wasn't sent here for nothing. Being found guilty on 714 counts of graffiti vandalism can hardly be called a simple brush with the law!

So giving him a can of paint again could have meant black marks for all of us. But no. Happily, this has not been the case. 281745 has responded well to the challenge and appears to have discovered a purpose in life.

He is a slow worker, but definitely getting faster. Whereas Michaelangelo's painting speed might once have been described as snail's-paced it is now noticeably quicker: more turtle-paced, I would say.

And, what is more, the school has gained from 281745's industry. Every wall, every window, every door...all now gleam with a fresh coat of paint.

Having angels on the toilet block ceiling is a bit unusual, but I suppose I'll get accustomed to them eventually.

Ike E. Pemin

Sgt. Ike E. Pemin
Head Warder

S T A R F L E E T
Secondary School

Name of Pupil: KIRK, James T.
Age: 13
Dateline: 19 January 2904
Subject: Leadership

This report is a mixture of good news and bad news.

The good news is that Kirk is a born leader.

The bad news is that Kirk acts as though he was born yesterday. This is reflected in the fact that the other trainees have nicknamed him James T. Berk.

For example, potential Starfleet Commanders do not charge into the girls' cloakroom bellowing at the tops of their voices, 'Come on, you lot! Let's boldly go where no lad has gone before!'

Neither do they rush out again, their eyes popping, and yell 'Cor! Gawp factor one!!'

One might be tempted to make allowances, and say that this is just a phasor Kirk is going through, were he not quite so insensitive to the feelings of others.

On the assault course the other day, for instance, Kirk was paired with another boy in a task which involved them both climbing on to a narrow plank of wood. The other boy was about to give Kirk a hand up when his nose started to run. A potential leader, sensitive to the needs of a member of his team, would have happily waited while the other boy took out his handkerchief. Not so Kirk. Even I, on the other side of the field, heard him scream, 'Come on, beam me up, Snotty!'

The future commander of a star ship? I wouldn't put him in charge of a star rowing boat.

Gail Force

Ms Gail Force
Chief Instructress

Cordon Bleu
Cookery School

Name of Pupil: BORGIA, Lucrezia
Age: 10
Subject: Cookery

I have found Lucrezia to be extremely moody during cookery classes. One minute she'll be as nice as pie, the next she'll have an attack of sour grapes. No wonder she doesn't seem to mix very well.

The other children certainly don't find Lucrezia's behaviour to their taste, and I can't say I blame them.

Last week I discovered her slipping some poisonous toadstools into Luigi Pettigrew's mushroom omelette. Talk about a recipe for disaster! If Luigi had taken it home his whole family would have had their chips.

Lucrezia's attitude to the incident I found particularly hard to stomach. I grilled her for some time about it and all I got in return was a lot of sauce. 'I couldn't care a fig,' she said. Well, I made it quite clear to Lucrezia that if she did anything like it ever again she'd really find herself in the soup. Hopefully that gave her food for thought.

Certainly she worked very hard on the jelly-making exercise I set this morning – without too much success, I'm sorry to say. Having just tasted Lucrezia's jelly I'm rapidly coming to the conclusion that she has little aptitude (or should I say apti-chewed, ha-ha!) for cookery. Her jelly has a most peculiar flav-aaaaaaaagggggghh...!

R.I.P. Hot-Pot

Mrs R.I.P. Hot-Pot
(signed in her absence).

Strike-A-Light

School for Nurses

Name of Pupil: NIGHTINGALE, Florence

Age: 16

Subject: Basic Nursing

Does Florence have trouble with her eyesight? It's the only explanation I can think of to account for her extremely poor performance in this subject.

Take her method of finding out what's wrong with young children, for instance: whacking them in various places and asking 'does it hurt there?' is no substitute for actually *looking* for symptoms. Poor little Walter Nitt is just one example. Admittedly Florence did a quite beautiful job of putting his broken leg in plaster, but the fact remains that Walter only came in to have his verruca scraped. And then to ask the poor boy's parents for five pounds, claiming that 'all breakages must be paid for' was to add insult to injury.

Poor eyesight might also explain the terrible mix-up when I gave Florence two other simple jobs: firstly to dab some ointment on Milly Ming's gnat bites with cotton wool, and then to give some of the school's rusty pipework a good rubbing down with wire wool. The result was disastrous. The cotton wool made absolutely no impression on the pipework, and as for poor Milly's gnat bites...

Maybe Florence needs help to see things more clearly - a pair of spectacles, perhaps, or a lamp to light the way. Yes, a lamp would be most appropriate. She's certainly been getting on my wick.

Anna Sthetic

Anna Sthetic
Sister (no relation)

PYRAMIDS
PRIMARY SCHOOL

Name of Pupil: Tutankhamun

Age: 5

Subject: Kingship

Dear Pharoah,

I am sorry to report that Tutankhamun is a bit of a Mummy's boy.

He bawls for her whenever he falls over, which seems to be quite often. And does he make a fuss! Trying to soothe him by saying something like, 'Tut-Tut, Tut' does no good at all. The only thing that will ever calm him down is putting a bandage on whatever part of his body he's complaining about. The slightest cut or bruise, and on goes another layer.

I've had to warn him, 'If you're not careful, Tut, one day you'll have so much bandage wrapped round you that you won't be able to move. Then you'll have to stay here for ever!'

Unfortunately that only makes him worse. Then he runs off and locks himself in the Wendy Sarcophagus with his toys.

I tell you, Pharoah, he'll do that once too often. One day I'll leave him there. That'll give him something to sphinx about.

Yours sincerely,

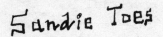

Sandie Toes, Playschool Leader

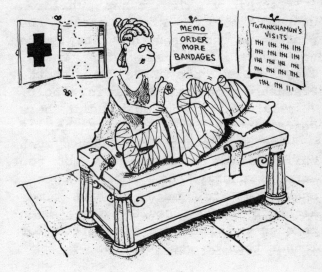

TOUCHDOWN
SCHOOL

Name of Pupil: TERRESTRIAL, Extra
Age: Not known - estimate, 13 billion
years.

Dear Mr and Mrs Terrestrial,
    I do so hope that your son,
Extra, enjoyed his stay with us as a
visiting scholar.
    Certainly the other children
enjoyed having Extra about the
place. As children do, they made
up their own name for Extra.
They called him E.T. for short.
Presumably because Extra is. Short,
I mean. Well, you must admit he's
certainly not extra large! Ha-ha!
    Whether or not E.T. learned much
while he was with us, I'm not too
sure. Frankly he looked rather
spaced-out for much of the time,
although that could have been
through being Saturn his bottom for
longer than he was used to.

Certainly he discovered a taste for chocolate. It was most unusual to see him without a Mars bar in his hand. Unless he was eating a Galaxy bar, of course. Or a Milky Way. I know for sure that he's spent most of his money. When I asked how much he'd got left he just shrugged and said 'Astro-nought'.

Finally, I hope he's returned home with all of his baggage. On his last morning here I found him in a distressed state, searching around in the woods at the back of the school. I asked him what he was looking for. 'Sputnik,' he croaked. Well, I called the whole school together and gave them all a rocket, but to no avail. Unfortunately I don't know what a sput looks like; if I had, it might have made it easier to find out who nicked it.

Yours sincerely,

I. Blastoff
Headmaster

CANAAN
SCHOOL FOR BOYS

Name of Pupil: JOSEPH, son of Jacob
Age: 17

Dear Jacob,

For the past few days your son, Joseph, has been attending school wearing a coat of many colours.

I have to remind you that this is expressly forbidden. The rule concerning school uniform is quite clear. All pupils shall wear a blazer in the school colours, khaki with olive green trim, available from the official stockist, Canaan Clothing.

Your adherence to this rule would be greatly appreciated.

Yours faithfully,

Jean Levi

Jean Levi
Head Mistress

Inter-Galactic

Middle School

Name of Pupil: VADER, Darth
Age: 9
Subject: Social skills

Darth is an enthusiastic pupil, but he must try to get on better with other boys.

On a number of occasions this term I have had to speak severely to him about his intolerant and unruly behaviour.

The incident concerning poor Lemuel Moon was a case in point. Admittedly the boy is rather slow - which is presumably why the other boys call him The Fool Moon - but, nevertheless, Darth could have had more patience with him during their joint classwork exercise to draw up a plan for the complete annihilation of the planet Earth. For Darth to cleave poor Moon in two with his junior laser-beam sword because he hadn't managed to calculate how many light years it would take to reach Trafalgar

Square was, in my opinion, something of an over-reaction.

Darth also responds poorly to constructive criticism. When I said to him, at the time of the Lemuel Moon incident, 'Two wrongs do not make a right,' his reply left much to be desired. Not only did he give me a very black look, he pointed at the two halves of the unfortunate Moon and said, 'No Sir, they make a right and a left!' I thought that reply was quite uncalled for, and told Darth so.

I still find it hard to forgive him for his petulant reaction. Slicing off my ear was extremely foolish. Had he been in any other class he would most certainly have had a slap on the back of his leg for that.

However, I remain convinced that his naughty behaviour is simply a mask, and that beneath it there's a friendly little fellow trying to get out. Perhaps he needs a regular playmate? A new boy, Luke Skywalker, joins us next term. Perhaps they will get on well together.

Obi-One-Kinobi-Two

Obi-One-Kinobi-Two
Form Master

WESTMINSTER
SKY HIGH SCHOOL

Name of Pupil: FAWKES, Guy
Age: 12

Dear Mr and Mrs Fawkes,

I'm afraid a rather unpleasant
incident blew up today involving
your son, Guy.

As you may be aware, today was our
Open Day. Guy's task was to meet
visitors arriving by car, and to
guide them quickly to the official
parking areas. Once there, he was to
collect a 25p parking fee, in aid of
school funds.

I'm sorry to tell you that Guy
quite flagrantly disobeyed these two
simple rules.

Firstly, he did not guide visitors
quickly. On one occasion I followed
him as he led a rather ancient car

to the parking area. He positively dawdled, spending most of the time chatting idly to the driver about his vehicle. For instance, I distinctly heard him say, 'I bet it goes like a bomb.' The boy was talking nonsense - the thing was a dreadful old banger.

Worse was to come, however. When finally they arrived at the parking spot your son not only took the 25p fee but asked for a tip! Again, I heard it with my own ears. Holding out his hand he asked, 'Penny for the guide, mister?'

I exploded, I'm afraid, and told Guy that his behaviour was deplorable. I hope you agree with me and trust that you, too, will give him a piece of your mind. It will do him no harm at all to get another rocket.

Yours sincerely,

B. Feater
Headmaster.

St.Nicholas'
Primary School

Name of Pupil: SCROOGE, Ebenezer
Age: 5

Dear Mr and Mrs Scrooge,

I am afraid that little Ebenezer had something of an upset at school today and I thought it only proper that you should be told precisely what happened.

As is traditional on the last day of the term before Christmas, our infant class enacted the Nativity Story. Ebenezer was playing Joseph, and pretty Alice Cringeworm was Mary.

Now, all went well until Ebenezer approached the door of the Inn. That was when the trouble began.

You see, the innkeeper was being played by that dirty ragamuffin Archie Gobbs. I'd been doubtful about him in rehearsals and, in the event,

I was right. The wretched boy hadn't learnt his lines. Thus, the dialogue went something like this:

JOSEPH (EBENEZER): My wife, Mary, is with child. Have you got any room at your inn?
INNKEEPER (GOBBS): No. Buzz off.
JOSEPH (EBENEZER): How about the stable? Could we use that?
INNKEEPER (GOBBS): No. You'll frighten the oxos.
JOSEPH (EBENEZER): Don't you mean yes?
INNKEEPER (GOBBS): No, I mean no! Sling yer hook, Scroogie-boy.
JOSEPH (EBENEZER): You've got it all wrong . . .
INNKEEPER (GOBBS): Oh yeh! Take that!

And to my horror the dreadful boy punched poor little Ebenezer on the nose!

Not unnaturally, Ebenezer became quite upset at this point and ran off (stage right, if my memory serves me correctly) and locked himself in the boys' toilets. Sobbing his little heart out for two hours, he was. By then it was all over. The play had finished, the Christmas party had ended (not a scrap of jelly left in sight of course, little pigs) and Father Christmas was about to leave for home. All he had left in his sack for Ebenezer was a bag of sweets. Humbugs, I believe.

Again, I can only express my sincere apologies for what happened. I do hope it doesn't put Ebenezer off Christmas for ever.

Season's Greetings,

Holly Ivy
Form Mistress

YE
LONDINIUM ACADEMIE
FOR YOUNGE LADIES

Name of Pupil: Boadicea
Age: 12

Report for summer term, AD 48

BEHAVIOUR

Boadicea may be younge, but she is certainly no ladie.

She is wilde and verie verie pignacious. She is alwayes so determined to get her owne way that she spends more time in ye academie's dungeons than she does in ye classeroomes.

I do not think Boadicea has learnte anything at all in her time here. Not even to spelle here owne name, whiche the sillie girle still writes as Boudicca.

SUBJECT REPORTS

Embroiderie

Boadicea woulde not do ye lace doilie classe work. She spente all her time in embroiderie of ye backe of here leathere jacket with suche slogans as, 'Boudicca rools, OK?' and 'Worlde Tour, AD 48, Boudicca and ye Battlers'.

Cookerie

Dreadfulle. The onlie time Boadicea showed an intereste was in ye lesson about howe to make chippes. Even then she onlie wanted to boile ye oile. When I asked her what she had to putte in it nexte she did not knowe. All she coulde saye was, 'Do not worrie, Miss, I will thinke of some-bodie.'

I was not amusede. Neither was Esmerelda Pike, who was the somebodie she thoughte of.

Handiecraft

Boadicea forsooke ye basketrie option in favoure of ye metalworke. Lo and beholde, ye academie chariot, used for alle mannere of outings, suddenlie findes itself with a razore-sharpe sworde-blade on eache wheelie.

Ye chariote dulie failed its MOT test. True, it is olde; true, it may have failed ye test anywaye; but ye examiner having his legges cutte off at ye knees did not helpe a bitte.

Franklie, I thinke it woulde be

bettere for alle concerned if Boadicea lefte ye academie as soone as possible. The careeres officer sayes there is a good war coming up and they wille wante all ye lunatiks they can gette.

Bettie Smithe

Bettie Smithe
Forme Teachere

WILD WEST
VILLAGE SCHOOL

Name of Pupil: DAN, Desperate
Age: 15

Dear Mr and Mrs Dan,

As we all know, Desperate is not a bright boy (if boy is the right word for someone who's been shaving since he was six). He has spent so long at the bottom of the class the other children call him 'Shipwreck'.

It therefore gives me great pleasure to write and tell you that Desperate has finally managed to come top of the class in a General Knowledge test!

I know how delighted you must be at this news of his success, so I'm enclosing Desperate's completed exam paper.

This was a tremendous performance, deserving of some reward - I'd give him a tenth helping of cow pie if I were you.

Yours sincerely,

Spike Cactus

Spike Cactus
Head Teacher

General Knowledge Test Paper

Q. What is the technical term detectives use to describe burglaries in which the crook has got away without leaving fingerprints?
A. Haven't got a clue.

Q. What is the word we use when a student has been successful in the examinations?
A. Pass.

Q. What does encore mean?
A. And again.

Q. Where does milk come from?
A. And anudder one.

Q. What does S.O.S. mean?
A. Help!

Q. What would a mountaineer be likely to say when the prevailing weather conditions prevented him from seeing where the peak was?
A. Haven't got the foggiest.

Q. What did the junior Dalek say when the Boss Dalek asked where the Tardis had gone?
A. Who knows.

GENOA
COMPREHENSIVE SCHOOL

Name of Pupil: COLUMBUS, Christopher
Age: 15

Dear Mr and Mrs Columbus,

My sincere apologies for the very late arrival home of your son Christopher following our school outing yesterday to the Genoa Country Park.

The cause of our delayed departure was, I am afraid, Christopher himself.

After lunch, all pupils were distributed with maps of the area and then allowed to explore. It took a search party three hours to locate Christopher after he got lost and failed to return at the appointed time.

I think it might be best, Mr and Mrs Columbus, if Christopher does not go on future outings of this type. He is an enthusiastic lad, but has absolutely no sense of direction.

Yours sincerely,

O. Whereami
Head of Geography

ROMA
GIRLS' SCHOOL

Name of Pupil: LISA, Mona
Age: 15

Mona is as pretty as a picture.

However, she is altogether too quiet. In fact, she seems to have very little life in her at all. Whereas the other girls can't wait to get out into the playground, Mona is perfectly content to stay sitting in class.

She hardly contributes to class discussions. Mona rarely offers an answer to a question and, if asked if she understands, will often just smile.

Quite frankly, this is beginning to irritate me. Mona will soon be leaving school and, if she wants to make her way in the world, she really must become more outward-going.

Sitting for hours with a stupid grin on your face is not the way to become famous.

Iva Frame

Senorita Iva Frame
Form Mistress

GOTHAM CITY
Secondary School

Name of Pupil: GRAYSON, Dick
Age: 15

Attn. Mr Bruce Wayne, Guardian

Dear Mr Wayne,

I am writing to you to express my concern over the eccentric behaviour of your youthful ward, Dick Grayson.

He seems to be terribly excitable. Hardly a day goes by without my hearing about some new and curious thing he has said or done. For example:

* In Drama, he had to write an essay on the opening scene in Hamlet in which the three witches are huddled around their cauldron on a bleak Scottish moor. What did he hand in? Two words: 'Shivering Shakespeare!'

* He gave the school dentist a terrible shock when she examined him after he complained of a sore

mouth. To have your patient leap
out of the chair screaming 'Great
Galloping Gumboils!' is not funny.

★ It is also most disconcerting for
the dinner ladies, when expecting
a simple choice from the menu, to
be met by a wild-eyed youth who
slams a fist into the palm of his
hand and screams things like 'Holy
Hamburgers', or 'Fantasmagorical
French Fries' at the top of his
voice.

Until now I have overlooked these
incidents, preferring to put them
down to youthful exuberance. I have
even turned a blind eye to Dick's
strange desire to wear motorcycling
gauntlets in class. But what
happened today I cannot ignore.

Mr Wayne, I will not have your ward
walking the hallowed corridors
of Gotham City School with his
underpants on over his trousers.

Yours sincerely,

Chuck M. Out

Chuck M. Out
Headmaster

TRAINING UNIT
Assembly Line 18b

Name of Pupil: DALEK, No ACK-231-Q-897654449Z
Age: 6 minutes

This is to certify that ACK-231-Q-897654449Z (hereinafter referred to as 'ACK') has completed a course of extermination training and achieved a satisfactory standard.

Assessments obtained in individual elements of the course were as follows:

MOVEMENT: Generally smooth, but suffered from the odd squeak. Could have sent ACK back, but instead sent ACK to the Quack. Problem resolved by a dose of caster oil. Congratulated doctor who said, 'Where there's a wheel, there's a way.'

HEAD ROTATION: Excellent. ACK has the knack.

RECOGNISING THE ENEMY: Problems at first, with two fellow Daleks, ZAK and MAC, mistakenly subjected to an ACK-attack. Difficulty overcome by scientific means. Gave ACK a whack on the back. ACK can now spot humanoids, particularly humanoids daft enough to wear bright clothes and long multi-coloured scarves, without any need to ask 'Who?'

TAKING ORDERS: Very good. Responds immediately and without question; i.e. no ACK-yak-back.

SPEECH: Spoke first word after 2.41 seconds. It was, of course, 'Exterminate!' Anything else and it would have been the sack for ACK.

EXTERMINATION: Able to exterminate the enemy from behind, from the side and from the front. A good all-rounder, in other words. Did very well in all gun techniques - laser gun, stun gun, bubble gun (good for stick-ups) - but especially ack-ack gun.

ACK-231-Q-89765449Z shows great promise. With normal progress ACK should reach the level expected of a TV performer within 40 million years.

Dalek AA - aaaaaaaaaaaa2 -A

Dalek AA-00000000002-A
Senior Destructor Instructor

Fairy Godmother

Girls' School

Name of Pupil: Cinderella
Age: 17

Dear Baron Hardup,

Yet again, Cinderella has fallen asleep at her desk.

That makes the third time this week, and the twenty-first time this month. (And she snores so loudly! Any husband she might eventually win for herself won't find that too charming). This really must stop.

Clearly, she is not getting enough sleep. But why? As her personal counsellor I felt it incumbent upon me to find out. This is why I am writing to you. Having spoken at length to Cinderella (when she woke up) I fear that we are dealing with a much bigger problem than simple insomnia.

I suspected as much when she said that the usual cause of her tiredness was the vast amount of castlework - scrubbing, cleaning, polishing Buttons etc – that, she claims, her delightful sisters force her to do.

But when she told me the reason why she was especially tired today... Well, I was left in no doubt. My dear sir, it is my unpleasant duty to tell you that Cinderella is – to put it bluntly – stark raving bonkers.

What other explanation can there be, when a girl claims that she didn't get to bed until after midnight because she had to hop all the way home from a glittering ball wearing one glass slipper, due to the coach she arrived in having turned into a giant pumpkin! I ask you – what a whopper!

I'm sorry, but I think we should meet to discuss some treatment for the girl. I only wish I could wave a magic wand and sort her out myself.

Yours despairingly,

U. What!

Ms U. What
Counsellor

WILDERNESS
Outward Bound School

Name of Pupil: MOSES
Age: 18
Subject: Orienteering

Moses is a born leader. Under his captaincy the school's orienteering squad has gone from strength to strength.

Last week's final of the Cleopatra Trophy was the high-point of the season. It's always a needle match when the Cleopatra Trophy is at stake, but even more so against the Pharoah's select squad.

Nobody who watched what happened will ever be able to forget Moses' brilliance.

Admittedly we had a little luck to begin with. By all accounts the Pharoah's squad were plagued with injuries in the days leading up to the match, though whether you can believe all you read in the papyruses is another matter. Claims that their training had been badly disrupted by swarms of

locusts and hordes of frogs sounded a
bit far-fetched to me, but there was no
denying that the loss of Pharoah's son
through a sudden dose of death was a
serious blow to them.

At the end of the day though, the
orienteering title still had to be won,
and it was Moses we had to thank for
our crushing victory. His tactics were
absolutely outstanding.

Heading off while the Pharoah's lot
were still asleep was a crafty move. It
gave us a head start before the sun
came up. That became very important
when they finally got under way.

They'd solved all the clues and were
catching us fast. Too fast for my
liking. Frankly - and I can admit it
now - I thought Moses had got it wrong.
Coming to the water obstacle, I really
thought we were going to lose.

That was when Moses showed his class.
How he managed to judge it I don't
know, but no sooner had our team got
across than the tide came in.
Absolutely amazing. It certainly left
the Pharoah's team in a lot of trouble

(up the creek without a paddle, as one might say) and there we were, high and dry - champions!

Terrific stuff, and all down to Moses. I wish him all the best as he leaves us and goes, I don't doubt, on to higher things. (Excuse the feeble joke - I refer to his mountaineering abilities of course). What with his all-round sporting acumen and his practical talents at masonry and stone-carving, he seems destined to reach the very top.

I. Walkabout

I. Walkabout
Games Master

MELCHESTER ROVERS
Soccer Academy

Name of Pupil: RACE, Roy
Age: 14
Subject: Football

Footballers is supposed to be intelligents but this here pertikuler RACE is lost.

He spends most of his tyme imajining himself in the furst team scoring goalls left, right and centre spot. 'Roy of the Rovers', he calls himself. Well I's sorry if what I've gotto rite will disappoint the lad, but my oppoonion is he ain't not got a chance.

There's too much competition here, see. I mean like, Race ain't as fast as that young Gary Spinnaker – goes like the wind that boy. Niver is his ball control nuffink like as good as Chris Doddle's (he makes it all look so easy), or his tackling as hard as y'know, Vinnie Bones, who's broken a few in his time. I mean, Race doesn't even smile much, not like our goalie keeper Peter Stilton who's always got a cheesey grin on his face.

No, the only fing about Race what stannds out is his redd hair. I knows that'll disappoint the boy and naturolly he'll feel as sick as a carrot.

Wally Overthemoon

Wally Overthemoon
Yoof Teem Couch

BAKER STREET
COMPREHENSIVE

Name of Pupil: HOLMES, Sherlock
Age:9

Dear Mr and Mrs Holmes,

I write to inform you that you will
shortly be receiving a visit from an
extremely angry Bow Street Runner. He
will be asking you to knock some sense
into your cretinous son, Sherlock.

Why? Because today, after employing
what the boy fancifully calls his
'powers of deduction' on a man who just
happened to be passing the classroom
window, Sherlock apparently ran to the
nearest telephone and summoned the
Baker Street Constabulary. 'Come
immediately,' he told them, 'a mass
murderer is on the loose!'

Within minutes a horde of armed
policemen had descended on the school
and arrested the man who, it transpired,
was perfectly innocent of any crime.
Only then was your son's part in this

dreadful waste of police time and
public money fully revealed.

The man in question walked with a
limp. He was also sporting a carnation
in his buttonhole, carrying a newspaper
under his arm and, at the instant he
was unfortunate enough to be spotted by
your son Sherlock, had been in the act
of picking his nose.

As far as I have been able to
determine, the following conversation
then took place between Sherlock and
the numbskull who sits next to him in
class, a boy named Watson:

HOLMES: Watson! That man is a mass
   murderer!
WATSON: Good Lord, Holmes! Why?
HOLMES: The carnation in his buttonhole
   for a start. Carnations are out of
   season, Watson. It must be worth a
   fortune which he, as a poor man,
   cannot have. He must have stolen it.
WATSON: Blooming brilliant, Holmes!
   But how on earth do you know he's
   poor?
HOLMES: The limp. An industrial injury,
   if I'm not mistaken, which would
   leave him out of work to boot...and
   desperate, as the rolled-up newspaper
   reveals!

WATSON: Newspaper? Holmes, I know
  you're the Star Mail of our Times
  Today, Sun, but why?
HOLMES: Observer-ation, my dear Watson.
  He's been checking it to find out
  if the police are hunting for a
  dangerous carnation-thief who has
  committed mass murder!
WATSON: Murder? Holmes, you've lost
  me...
HOLMES: The man is picking his nose
  with his little finger, Watson. Most
  people use their index finger. Why
  isn't he?
WATSON: Haven't got a clue.
HOLMES: Because his index finger must
  be badly injured, of course!
  Conclusive evidence that he has
  recently fired a heavy pistol a
  number of times!

The fact that the poor man was
responding to an advertisement in the
newspaper for a school gardener,
whose carnation was evidence of his
gardening ability, and whose limp
was due to his having dropped a fork
on his foot when he dug up the
carnations, appears not to have been
an option that your son considered.
Nor the fact that not everybody

picks their nose with their index
finger.

Doubtless the Sergeant will explain
this at great length to Sherlock when
he calls.

Yours sincerely,

Jim Berger-Whack

Jim Berger-Whack
Headmaster

SHERWOOD FOREST
SENIOR SCHOOL

Name of Pupil: HOOD, Robin
Age: 14
To: The Under-Sheriff, Town Hall,
Nottingham.

Dear Sir,
I am in receipt of your letter
requesting a character reference for
Robin Hood, prior to his forthcoming
appearance before you at the
Magistrates Court on 87 charges of
demanding money with menaces.

Much as it grieves me to admit
such a thing about a pupil of this
school, I can find virtually nothing
to say in Hood's defence. The boy is
a thoroughly nasty piece of work.

Despite countless floggings,
Hood's gang of thugs — they call
themselves Hoodlums, I understand —
has terrorised the junior pupils for
as long as I can remember.

I expect that their names are
already well known to your juvenile
delinquent department: the boy John
Little, for instance, enjoys nothing
better than whacking first-formers

behind the ear with that wooden stave he carries everywhere; and the fat boy Tuck, of course, can empty another lad's sandwich box in the twinkling of an eyelid.

Hood is the worst, though. I had hoped that he was going to improve. A new girl seemed to have taken his eye and I thought that he might calm down. Quite the opposite, I am afraid; Marion just seems to have Maid him worse.

No, I am sorry my Lord-Under-Sheriff: the boy Hood is an unpleasant piece of boyhood. In my opinion you would be well advised to deal with him severely. A few thousand hours community service, clearing litter from the forest, say, is what he needs.

Yours faithfully,

Ivy Greenwood

I.V. Greenwood
Headmaster

P.S. Do not be fooled by Hood's usual story, that he robs the rich to give to the poor. He's had money off some of the richest little herberts in this school and he's never given me a penny of it.

Stratford-on-Avon
Grammar School

Name of Pupil: SHAKESPEARE, William

Age: 16

Subject: English

Never in my whole career have I met a boy as hopeless at English as Shakespeare. He hasn't got a clue.

A failure in the forthcoming examinations is an absolute certainty, and for one very good reason. The boy seems incapable of giving a straight answer to a straight question.

Consider the following, the first line from a recent essay:

'To be, or not to be, that is the question...'

Complete and utter poppycock. That was not the question. The question, which I wrote on the board very clearly was, 'Write an essay

of 400 words entitled "What I did on my
Holidays"'

Frankly, I rarely understand a single word
Shakespeare writes. For instance, in his essay
'What I Got From Father Christmas', he
wanted to say that Santa didn't bring him
everything he had on his stocking list. But
could he express that simple idea in a straight-
forward manner? He could not. His essay
began:

'Now is the winter of our discontent...'

And again, in the mock examinations, he
was required to use his imagination and describe
a day in the life of somebody working in an
hotel. What happens? He makes a good start,
choosing to describe what a chef does. Then
what does the idiot produce as an opening line?

'Double, double toil and trouble; fire burn
and cauldron bubble...'

In an essay called 'What Life Would Be
Like Without Pocket-Money' I encountered:

'Friends, Romans, countrymen; lend me
your ears...'

The examples are endless. All, I am afraid, lead one to the inevitable conclusion: that Shakespeare's writing is completely and utterly incomprehensible. Certainly I cant't understand it.

Amazingly, I believe the boy wants to write plays when he leaves school. The very thought is too awful to contemplate. Can you imagine what it would be like if his work found its way into the classroom and some poor teacher had to try and explain what it was all about? The mind boggles.

I. McBeth

I. McBeth
Head of English

INNER JUNGLE
EDUCATION AUTHORITY
STEAMING SWAMP SCHOOL

Name of Pupil: TARZAN

Age: 13

Dear Mr and Mrs Orang-Utan,

I write to you in your capacity as guardians of young Tarzan.

Please would you ensure that, with a single exception, Tarzan refrains from bringing his animal friends to school.

The pride of lions have caused nothing but trouble. Recruiting good pupils is difficult enough as it is. Having them eaten by your son's pets does absolutely nothing to help. Today, little John Silver was attacked. Compared to previous victims, he was lucky: he only had his leg bitten off. Bang go his chances in the area sports 100 metres, though. We'll just have to put the poor chap in for the invitation hopscotch event instead.

Assuming, of course, that the field can be cleared in time for the sports to take place. Tarzan's elephant - the one he rides to school - has been up to his old tricks again. The groundsman is going to have to work all night to clean up the mess - once we've dug him out, that is. (The groundsman's going to have to go as well; he's always putting his foot in it).

No, Tarzan must leave his lions and elephants at home. And his boa constrictor, the giraffe, the crocodile ... all except the chimpanzee.

The chimpanzee can stay. It would be silly to forbid Tarzan to bring all his pets, and the chimpanzee is no trouble. Besides, it came top in the exams.

Yours sincerely,

Tom Tom

Tom Tom
Head Teacher

RICHARD DUSZZAK.

CANAAN
SCHOOL FOR BOYS

Name of Pupil: JOSEPH, ex-son of Jacob
Age: 17

Dear Jacob,

May I say how sorry I was to hear that your son Joseph had been eaten by wolves and his coat of many colours torn to shreds.

I am pleased to see that your eleven other sons are taking the loss of Joseph well, also that they are dressed in regulation school uniform.

Perhaps if Joseph had been similarly dressed he would still be with us today. To my certain knowledge, wolves have never torn to shreds any pupil wearing a blazer of khaki with olive green trim.

I can only imagine that Joseph's outfit made the wolves see red. And yellow, and blue...

Yours sincerely,

Jean Levi

Jean Levi
Head Mistress

NOTRE DAME
JUNIOR SCHOOL

Name of Pupil: QUASIMODO
Age: 11
Subject: Physical Education

Quasimodo is a talented gymnast. A genuinely bouncy character, he seems equally at home on all items of apparatus.

His speciality, however, has to be the ropes. Never, in all my years as a Games Master, have I seen a boy who could climb as quickly as Quasimodo; nor, for that matter, be capable of swinging from one side of the gymnasium to the other without touching the ground in between. Needless to say, he has been unbeatable at 'Pirates' this term.

All in all an excellent term's work, with only one small quibble.

On occasion, probably because Quasimodo is such an enthusiast, he has stayed on the ropes long after the other boys have gone off for their next lesson. Being ordered to come down has clearly left him in a bad mood for the rest of the day.

It is important for Quasimodo to learn that, much as he would like to, he cannot just swing around all day ignoring the bells; he must come down when he's told, and not get the hump about it.

Jim Nasium

Jim Nasium
Games Master

PLYMOUTH HO!
School for Naval Children

Name of Pupil: RALEIGH, Walter
Age: 5

Dear Mr and Mrs Raleigh,

This note is to explain why Walter has come home with a sopping wet blazer.

Having lost the toss with Miss Witherington, I was on playground duty this morning. Now, not surprisingly after the torrential rain we've been having over the past few days, the playground was covered with puddles.

Walter, I noticed, was over by the sand-pit, playing dolls with Elizabeth Shrimp. When the bell went they came skipping back to class, only to find the way barred by a particularly large puddle.

I would not have believed what happened next had I not seen it with my own eyes.

Instead of going round the puddle, Walter took off his blazer and laid it down for Elizabeth to tread on.

The condition of Walter's blazer, therefore is entirely the result of his own stupidity. Of course his sandwiches, geometry set, champion conker, Swiss pen-knife and miniature bowls set — all of which were in the pockets — are in the same soggy condition.

Yours sincerely,

Ms. R. Mada
Playground Supervisor

P.S. You should also expect to receive a bill from Mr and Mrs Shrimp in the next few days. Stupidly, Walter pulled his blazer away before Elizabeth stepped off it, with the result that she ended up flat on her back in two inches of mud and slime. In the circumstances, her screech of 'You great Wally' was perfectly understandable.

Hi-Ho House
Girls' School

Name of Pupil: WHITE, Snow
Age: 17

To: Doc, Happy, Sneezy, Dozey,
Grumpy, Sleepy and Bashful
Copy to: Area Education Officer

Dear Dwarves,

Truancy is not a little thing, it is
a very serious business.

Your explanation for Snow White's
continued absence from school, namely
that you haven't been able to wake
her up for forty years, is just not
good enough.

Have you thought of buying an alarm
clock?

Yours faithfully,

Faery Lightfoot

Mrs Faery Lightfoot
Headmistress

P.S. Thank you for the small gift.
An apple for the teacher is always
appreciated.

TOWER HAMLETS
MEDICAL SCHOOL

To: Professor I.N. Stitches,
Head of Medical School
Name of Pupil: JEKYLL (Dr, Trainee)
Age: 17

Jekyll has got what it takes to become
a very successful doctor with pots of
money.

He demonstrates a rattling good
knowledge of the sort of pills what us
chaps in the medical profession need to
dish out by the bucketful so's our
patients think we know what's wrong
with them. Also his prescription
writing is getting more and more
unreadable every day. Good progress,
indeed.

Even more encouragingly, Jekyll is
starting to invent pills and potions
of his own. This is excellent. Really

rich patients will cough up (ha-ha!) loadsamoney if you tell them they're shovelling a designer medicine down their throats rather than the sort of jollop anybody can pick up from chain stores chemists such as Wellington's.

The thing Jekyll has got to be careful about is trying the stuff on himself. Experiments with the new mixtures must be carried out on real patients, the nearer death's door the better - that way you can't be blamed if your stuff pops them off instead of getting them better.

As you know, I never recommend that students try their own potions. I mean, who knows what could happen? Certainly not us.

Q. Uack

Q. Uack (Doctor)
Lecturer in Medicine

GATH PLAY SCHOOL
PHILISTINE

Name of Pupil: GOLIATH

Age: **4**

Dear Mrs G.,

This is the customary letter that I write to parents of new pupils after they've been here at playschool for a month. I always write it after one month, even when it seems as though it's been like a year.

Goliath is a big boy for his age, isn't he? At 3 cubits and a span, he is twice as tall as most of the other little boys and girls we have here at play school. In fact he's taller than most of the helpers too.

Unfortunately, Goliath has started to use his size to get his own way. This morning, he gave little Bathsheba Benjamin a jolly hard push, just because she was ahead of him in the queue for mid-morning orange juice. At least, I think it was Bathsheba he pushed. The hole in the playschool wall was definitely shaped like her.

Goliath also got in the most frightful temper when he wasn't allowed to play in the Wendy House. With a single blow of his hand he smashed the thing to pulp. I was not pleased. Neither was Wendy, who was sitting inside at the time.

I do hope Goliath isn't becoming a bully. As he is continually being told, a nice boy doesn't pick on children smaller than himself. Perhaps he will grow out of it.

Anyway, he's not our only problem child. A little boy named David started last week, and he's an absolute terror. At least Goliath doesn't throw stones.

Yours sincerely,

April Showers

April Showers
Play Group Leader

METROPOLIS
JUNIOR HIGH SCHOOL

Name of Pupil: KENT, Clark
Age: 9

Clark is a mild-mannered boy. Nothing seems to make him angry, not even sitting next to Lois Lane all day. I certainly couldn't stand it, I know that. The girl never stops talking.

But is he accident-prone, by any chance?

I don't know what it is, but things just seem to collapse when Clark is around. He's crushed eleven chairs and four desks since he's been in my class.

Add to that six pieces of gymnasium equipment - including a set of wall bars which became floor bars when Clark swung on them, and a springboard which ended up in the basement when he jumped on it - and I am beginning to suspect that there's more to Clark Kent than meets the eye. Heavy bones, perhaps.

However, I have to say that his punctuality is excellent. He always arrives at school on time. How he does it, even when he misses the

school bus, I'm sure I don't know.
Whatever he does, he must really fly.

Marsha Mallow

Marsha Mallow
Form Mistress.

CITY OF ROME
Middle School

Name of Pupil: DA VINCI, Leonardo
Age: 12

GENERAL SCIENCE: Excellent

MATHEMATICS: Outstanding

PHYSICS: Outstandingly excellent

ASTRONOMY: Brilliant

ENGLISH: Completely brilliant

ART: Utterly brilliant, especially **PAINTINGS OF ENIGMATIC LADIES CALLED MONA LISA.**

BIOLOGY: Fantastic, especially **THINKING ABOUT WHY BLOOD STAYS INSIDE US MOST OF THE TIME AND GENERALLY FINDING OUT HOW BODIES WORK.**

INVENTING THINGS: Unbelievably brilliant, especially **INVENTING THINGS LIKE HELICOPTERS THAT NOBODY CAN UNDERSTAND, LET ALONE MAKE EVEN IF THEY HAD A BIG ENOUGH ELASTIC BAND.**

Leonardo obtained 100% in every exam, except for Biology in which he got 120% due to the fact that he finished so quickly he had time to set himself another question and answer that as well.

He always gets his homework in on time and is never late.

He has never had a day off because he was sick, because his Mum/Dad/Auntie/Dog was sick, because the horse wouldn't start, or for any other reason.

All things considered, Leonardo has a perfect record.

I just cannot understand why all the other children hate the sight of him.

Luigi Squeegee

Luigi Squeegee
Form Master.

SENATE

SECONDARY SCHOOL

Name of Pupil: CAESAR, Gaius Julius
Age: 13

Julius is at a difficult age.

Being born great is sometimes a considerable problem. It is very easy to slip into the belief that one is superior in every respect. Not to put too fine a point on it, one can become big-headed.

I have noticed a certain lack of modesty in Julius of late, even where relatively trivial demonstrations of his ability are concerned. For instance, his reaction to winning a couple of lunchtime matches of that game boys play with horse chestnuts on a length of string was terribly brash. He strutted into class, put his hands on his hips, and announced at the top of his voice 'I came, I saw, I conkered.'

Fortunately, however, he seems to be getting in with a good group of friends. This is most important when you're destined to be a great leader, as Julius clearly is. In politics, people are always ready to stab you in the back.

Julius will appreciate being surrounded by friends such as Mark Anthony and Brutus. Even the greatest men have bad days, but with loyal mates to talk to Julius won't feel too cut up about things for long.

Augustus Septemberus Octavius Headus

SCHOOL FOR THE SONS OF SECRET AGENTS

Name of Pupil: BOND, James
Age: 15

Dear Mr and Mrs Bond,

This school does its level best to provide meals with a high nutritional content. It makes available a wide and varied diet, to suit all tastes. It also offers a full range of beverages - tea, coffee, orange squash, lemon squash, fizzy lemonade, milk ..

What it does not offer is a full wining and dining service so that your son James can impress 3rd form girls like Pussy Wilkinson and Domino Dobson with his savoir faire.

Please make this point to him. Also that if he asks me just once more for an orange squash and lemonade cocktail, shaken not stirred, I will personally shove my serving spoon right up his hooter.

Winifred Moneypenny

Mrs Winifred Moneypenny
Dinner Lady

PUMPING METAL
COMPREHENSIVE SCHOOL

<u>Inter-schools</u> <u>Weightlifting</u>
<u>Tournament</u>

1st round match vs. Philistine Boys

Dear SAMSON,
I am pleased to tell you that you
have been selected for the School
Weightlifting Team, to compete in
the Inter-Schools Weightlifting
Tournament. For our first match we
are away to Philistine Boys.
Transport will be provided.

Please remember at all times
that you are representing your
school. For this reason we expect
team members to ensure that they are
smartly dressed with a collar and
tie; also (a point for you to note
especially), that their hair is
neatly trimmed.

Good luck!

I. Workout

I. Workout,
Games Master.

Hyperspace School
for Time-Travellers

Name of Pupil: WHO, Doctor
Age: 9

Dear Mr and Mrs Who,

Is there any chance that you could change your surname? Anything will do, so long as it's different. How about Rumplestiltskin or Ztipz? Qwertyuiop, perhaps, or Ng?

The reason is, you see, with your son being called what he is, I'm having terrible trouble every time I try to take the register. It invariably goes something like this...

- Kirk?
- Here, Miss.
- Spock?

- Absent, Miss.
- Anybody know where?
- Where no man has gone before,
  Miss.
- Who?
- Spock has, Miss.
- No, no. Who. Is Who here?
- What?
- Who! Is Who here?
- That's not proper English, Miss. You
  mean who is here?
- Well, is he?
- Who?
- Who!
- Oh, Who! Why didn't you say so,
  Miss? It's for you-Who!!
- Who me?
- YES, YOU WHO!!
- You're shouting again! You'll make
  me cry, Miss.
- No, don't ..
- I can't help it .. Waaagggh!
  Boo-who!!!

And so it goes on.

Please, Mr and Mrs Who, can you change your name? Register-taking would be so much easier without all this who-ha.

Yours sincerely,

[signature]

Lieutenant WhoWoora
Form Teacher

'ARROW SCHOOL

Name of Pupil: TELL, William
Age: 13
Subject: Archery

I have to Tell you that William is an absolute menace.

At first, he couldn't fire an arrow straight to save his life.

I'd tried him with a longbow and I'd tried him with a short bow. I'd tried him standing up straight and not bowing at all. Finally, when I was really annoyed, I tried him with a crossbow. Surprisingly, he found he was quite good with it.

The trouble is that now he'll aim at anything. At first he was content to go into the field behind the school and practise hitting bulls-eyes from forty paces. Then the farmer started to complain (the bulls weren't looking very cheerful either), and William had to turn his attentions elsewhere.

Since then I've found him intimidating first year pupils by shooting arrows into their cans of drink and shouting 'Yeh! Hole orange!'

I've also had complaints about him from the fatter boys in his class. Being threatened by somebody aiming an arrow at you and yelling 'Come on, quiver!' is not much fun.

Frankly, William is starting to give me the pip. Goodness knows what he'll try next.

Jeremy Archer

Jeremy Archer
Sports Master

TRANSYLVANIA
—TAP AND BALLET—
SCHOOL

Name of Pupil: FRANKENSTEIN

Age: 6

Dear Baron Frankenstein,

I have to be honest. Your creation will never become a dancer.

He tries hard, but he's got two left feet.

Yours sincerely,

A. Pirrouette

A. Pirrouette
Principal Instructor.

King Henry's School for Potential Wives

⟨⟩

Name of Pupil: BOLEYN, Anne
Age: 8
Subject: History

Anne is very keen on this subject. She's not as confident on her dates as she might be, but she certainly knows her Kings.

She enjoyed our outing to the Royal Palace. I had a lot of trouble dragging her away when the time came to go home. In the end I had to take her by the ear and say 'chop-chop' with some force. If the headmaster had been there, she'd have really got it in the neck.

We are hoping for great things for Anne in the forthcoming examinations. Her mother was also very good at history, and in this respect Anne is clearly a chip off the old block. Just so long as she doesn't lose her head and get carried away, she should obtain a good grade.

A.X.E. Mann

Mr A.X.E. Mann
Deputy Head

SCHOOL FOR SCARECROWS

Name of Pupil: GUMMIDGE, Worzel

Age: 12

Worzel is driving me up the pole, mainly because he's never up his.

He really must remember that he is a trainee scarecrow. If he doesn't work hard he'll find himself pulled to bits and his straws sold. I'm sure he wouldn't fancy finishing his days in a thousand milkshakes. That would be a very sticky end.

It's not as if he's stupid. He's not...well, at least not when his various heads are working properly. It's just that they seem to be stuffed with the wrong things.

Worzel's history head, for instance. It keeps on saying things like, 'History

isn't what it was, you know,' and
'History is out of date.' His Geography
head is a little bit better, but saying
things like 'Geography is where it's
at, man,' doesn't add much to class
discussion.

The worst time is when he's got his
witty head on. Then we get comments
like, 'Chemistry stinks' and 'Geometry
is for squares.' He was wearing it the
other day in the Maths lesson when I
told him he should ask if he got stuck,
not just sit there. And what was his
reply? 'I bet Pythagoras used to suck
his theorem.'

No, it's not good enough. Worzel has
got to try much harder if he wants to
get ahead.

I. Squawk

I. Squawk,
Crowman

COLISEUM
COMPREHENSIVE

Name of Pupil: HUR, Ben
Age: 13

CHARIOT-DRIVING PROFICIENCY BADGE

The results of the Chariot-Driving
Proficiency Test, which your son was
encouraged to take as part of last
term's Road Safety Campaign, are now
available.

I am sorry to say that Ben was not
successful. For your information, the
examiner's comments are reproduced
below.

BASIC CHARIOT MAINTENANCE: Poor. The
chariot's wheels were in a terrible
condition. Hur only spoke up when I
pointed this out to him. Then he
agreed with me that they were the hub
of the problem.

HORSE POWER: Inadequate. The chariot
was being pulled by his miserable

mother and three of his crotchety aunts. This was not good enough. Chariots are heavy vehicles, and need to be pulled by something better than four old nags.

CONTROL: Erratic. Went round every corner on one wheel, claiming that it made the tyres last twice as long. Regularly drove one-handed and sometimes no-handed. This was appalling. A good driver knows how important it is to take care in the rein.

CONSIDERATION FOR OTHER ROAD USERS: None at all. Ben regarded any faster-moving chariot's attempt to overtake as a personal insult, to be rebuffed by running the unfortunate driver through with his sword. When I asked him to justify this lack of tolerance, he said, 'It's called a duel carriageway, ennit?'

KNOWLEDGE OF THE HIGHWAY CODE: Non-existent. He thought a red traffic light meant that everything would stop for him, and his idea of a road sign was to shake his fist at anybody who didn't.

OVERALL PERFORMANCE: Quite dreadful. Mark my words, the boy is going to be in some very nasty pile-ups if his driving doesn't improve.

I can just see him ending up in hospital and the rest of us having to have a whip-round to buy him a present.

Fordus Escortus
Examiner

Ben Hur's horse power

PALM TREE
COMPREHENSIVE

Name of Pupil: CRUSOE, Robinson
Age: 12

5-day Survival Course

The course was designed to teach the boys how to survive on their own by living off the land for a week.

Robinson hated every minute of it. He showed no idea at all. Heaven knows how he'd cope if he ever did find himself stranded on a desert island. The only time he showed any enthusiasm at all was right at the end of the week.

Then he said, 'At last! It's Friday!'

Sandy Beach

Sandy Beach
Instructor (of Course)

Heaven High Higher High School

Name of Pupil: DEVIL, The
Age: Infinite

I hereby confirm that The Devil is expelled from Heaven for continued misbehaviour over a long period of time — ever since the school was created, in fact.

It is no exaggeration to say that he has made life absolute hell for us all.

The little misdemeanours, like turning up the school central heating system to full blast, or poking the headmaster in the backside with his three-pronged fork, were bad enough.

But his continued tormenting of other pupils cannot be forgiven. Grumbleweed, in the third form, was one of the worst cases. Devil had him boiled in oil, six days a week for a whole term. Even the point that Devil made to show his good side — that at least he'd allowed Grumbleweed out to play for the school rugby XV on Sunday mornings — was no defence whatsoever. Can you imagine what it was like playing rugby after being boiled in oil all week?

Yesterday's escapade was the final straw. All creatures in Heaven must be respected, that is the school rule. And yet Devil, in complete and utter disregard of this rule, killed one of the friendly sea-creatures in the school pond. Even worse, he extracted the creature's molars and ate them for his supper.

Enough! The Devil is expelled! Let him go to where such behaviour is tolerated — to where there is whaling and noshing of teeth.

St. Michael

St. Michael
Head of 5th Year (and School Outfitter
since 5 billion BC)

St. Peaceful's School for the Sons of Gentlefolk

Name of Pupil: JONES, Indiana
Age: 8

Dear Mr and Mrs Jones,

I understand that in order to get to school this morning Indiana leapt from the branches of a tree on to the roof of a passing vehicle, crawled the length of this vehicle (nearly falling off at least four times as he avoided having his head knocked off by low bridges), dangled precariously over the side - hanging on by the fingertips of one hand while he scratched his knee with the other - and then leapt fearlessly through a small side window, receiving not a single scratch in spite of the thousands of razor-sharp pieces into which the glass shattered.

Would you please instruct your son that he must be like all the other children, and use the school bus stop.

Ida Rather-Knot

Mrs Ida Rather-Knot
Form Mistress

NEPTUNE'S
SCHOOL FOR THE SONS
OF SAILORS

Name of Pupil: POPEYE
Age: 6

Dear Admiral Popeye,

I am sorry to tell you that your son
has been caught fighting in the playground yet again. And, once again, poor
little Bluto was the victim, with your
son being egged on by that big lump
Olive Oyl.

Frankly, Admiral, your son is a bad
influence. How many other 6-year-olds
have tattoos on their arms and smoke a
pipe? No wonder he has such a croaky
voice.

I have come to the conclusion that your
son's aggressive behaviour is something
to do with his diet. He's not eating
the right sort of food. I ask you,
spinach sandwiches every day! It can't
be good for him. Yes, I know you'll say

he gets two kilos of cream buns in his sandwich crate as well, but he doesn't touch those. They're all gobbled up by the already overweight Olive Oyl.

My strategy from now on is going to be simple. I'm going to give Popeye's spinach sandwiches and cream buns to weedy little Bluto. This should make all the difference. Popeye should stop being so aggressive and Olive Oyl get a lot thinner.

Whether or not there'll be any change in timid little Bluto remains to be seen.

Yours sincerely,

Arthur J. Swee'pea
Year Counsellor

Royal Surfing School
BEACHY HEAD

Name of Pupil: CANUTE
Age: 13

What can you do with a surfer who
spends all his time standing at the
water's edge telling the waves to go
back where they came from?
Absolutely nothing. Canute is a
big drip.

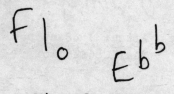

Miss Flo Ebb
Instructress

ACROPOLIS
BOYS' SCHOOL

Name of Pupil: PYTHAGORAS
Age: 15

Dear Mr and Mrs Pythagoras,

Please find enclosed a refund of all monies paid in respect of the school mountaineering expedition which we were forced to abandon yesterday.

Things had started so well, too.

Three guides were with us. Mr Potts, a very smartly-dressed man in a natty pair of tartan trews with matching tie, was our leader. He was already halfway up the side of a sheer slab of rock. His two fellow guides, whose names I never did learn, were standing next to me and explaining the finer points of climbing technique to the boys. That was when things started to go wrong.

Mr Potts was climbing so beautifully that I decided to get my telescope out for a closer look at his technique. Unfortunately however, in extricating said instrument from the depths of my haversack, I inadvertently poked its little end into the right eye of guide number 2.

He screamed in agony. That made me jump, as a consequence of which I then stuck the telescope's fat end into the left eye of guide number 3. He also began to scream and shout.

At that moment Mr Potts, no doubt wondering what all the hullabaloo was about, ignored his own advice and looked down. He promptly lost his footing and would have plummeted to certain death had his tie not become entangled in a thorn bush jutting out from a crack in the rock face.

By the time the ambulance had rushed guides 2 and 3 to hospital and the rescue services brought Mr Potts safely down to earth, there was no alternative but to abandon the expedition.

Yours sincerely

Cliff Face

Cliff Face,
Head of 5th Year

P.S. I have to say that Pythagoras' attitude during this episode was very disappointing.

Guides 2 and 3 were distinctly unhappy, of course, both having received a severe poke in one eye. Mr. Potts was in no laughing mood either, as he made perfectly plain even while hanging on to the rock face for all he was worth. It was a moment of considerable tension, with all three guides looking at me with what I can only describe as undisguised hatred.

All the more upsetting, therefore that your son Pythagoras should choose that moment to announce in a very loud voice, 'The glare on the high Potts in trews as the guide dangles tie-tangled is equal to the sum of the glares on the other two guides.'

CANAAN
SCHOOL FOR BOYS

Name of Pupil: JOSEPH, son of Jacob

Age: 39

Dear Jacob,

My heartiest congratulations on the return of your beloved son, Joseph!

To think that he'd been living in Egypt all the time!

I congratulate you, also, on your decision to send him back to Canaan School to continue his interrupted education. We are delighted to have him with us once again, and to hear his tales about life in Egypt.

Clearly the Pharoah treated him well! Nobody will kick sand in his face again! Joseph positively drips with gold, does he not? Gold cloak, gold bangles, golden sandals ... truly magnificent!

However, I must remind you that the
rule concerning school uniform is quite
clear. All pupils shall wear a blazer
in the school colours, khaki with olive
green trim, still available from the
official stockist (Canaan Clothing) or
most major department stores.

Your adherence to this rule would be
greatly appreciated.

Yours sincerely,

Jean Levi
Head Mistress

Once-upon-a-time
School for Girls

Name of Pupil: HOOD, Red Riding
Age: 6

Red Riding is a dreadful child –
almost as bad as her thieving
brother, Robin.

She is so insulting! Poor Esther
Ranter was reduced to tears the
other day when Red bellowed across
the classroom at her, 'What big
teeth you've got!'

And then there was little Kylie
Minnow. Being told, 'What a big
mouth you've got!' was bad enough,
but following up with 'It must be
some kind of record!' was just
awful. It sent the poor girl into a
flat spin.

Jason Bongovan got much the same
treatment. 'What funny clothes

you're wearing!' Red Riding cackled
at him yesterday. 'Where d'you get
'em from - the neighbours?'

Thankfully she's not staying for
lunch today. Red Riding showed me a
big basket of groceries and said she
was going to take them to her
Grandma.

Fat chance of that. Knowing her,
she's probably in the forest wolfing
them herself.

Amelia Bonecruncher

Amelia Bonecruncher
Form Mistress

Who's Really Who

Boadicea (or Boudicca) 36

An early feminist. An English Queen who led her gang into punch-ups with the inhabitants of villages like London.

Boleyn, Anne 93

Henry VIII's second wife, until she had her head chopped off. Then she became his axe-wife!!

Bond, James 84

Suave fictional spy, with tastes for good food and bad women. Favourite drink is a Martini, 'shaken, not stirred.' As if he could tell the difference.

Borgia, Lucrezia 20

Young lady with an unpleasant habit of slipping something nasty into the food of people she didn't like. All-in-all, a bit of a poisonous character.

Caesar, Julius   82

Emperor of Rome. Assassinated by his best
mates Brutus and Mark Anthony.

Canute   106

Dozy king, who tried to show he was in
charge by telling the waves to go away. Sea?

Cinderella   49

Pantomime character with a fairy godmother
whose ability to change household objects
into things like gold coaches enabled Cinders
to go to a glittering ball until the magic wore
off at midnight.

Columbus, Christopher   42

Italian navigator who discovered America
(not counting the millions of Americans who
were already living there, of course).

Crusoe, Robinson   100

Fictional character. Ended up on a desert
island without any discs but with a servant
named 'Man Friday'.

Dalek, No ACK-231-Q-897654492   47

Trundling enemy of Dr. Who in TV programme
of the same name, often given only one line in
the script – 'exterminate!'

Dan, Desperate   40

Appears in the comic, 'Dandy'. Has a very big body and a very little brain.

Da Vinci, Leonardo   80

Italian inventor, sculptor and general clever-dick.

Devil, The   101

Needs no introduction. A biblical character in fact, expelled from heaven.

Dracula, Count   10

Human vampire who never comes out during the day if he can help it. Gets very thirsty, causing him to bite human necks and drink their blood.

Fawkes, Guy   31

Tried to blow up the Houses of Parliament in 1605. Failed.

Frankenstein   92

Fictional monster, constructed by Baron Frankenstein out of spare parts removed from dead bodies without their permission.

Goliath   76

Biblical Big Daddy. Ended up losing the

heavyweight championship of Philistine to David and his catapult.

Grayson, Dick   45

Young man who, once he'd done his home-work, got changed out of his school uniform and turned into Batman's little mate, Robin.

Gummidge, Worzel   94

Fictional scarecrow, with a head for every occasion.

Holmes, Sherlock   56

Fictional detective, famous for solving cases through his amazing powers of deduction – amazing, that is, to his thicko of a pal, Dr Watson.

Hood, Red Riding   113

Fairytale character, plagued by a wolf who ate her grandmother and then dressed up in the old girl's clothes so that Red Riding Hood wouldn't recognise him before he had her for afters. This leads to classic dialogue between the two about size of teeth, mouth, ears etc, before the wolf gets mangled by a friendly woodcutter.

Hood, Robin   60

Legendary outlaw who lived in a semi-detached tree in Sherwood Forest with his mates Friar Tuck and Little John, and had his milk delivered by a lady named Maid Marion. Hobby: robbing the rich to give to the poor.

Hur, Ben   96
Title character of a film, in which Ben wins the climactic chariot race by a short head. Well, all the other heads had been shortened – mostly by losing their bodies.

Jekyll, Doctor   74
Fictional doctor who experimented on himself with a potion he'd invented. It turned him into a hairy horror called Mr Hyde, who spent his evenings bumping people off.

Jones, Indiana   103
Adventurous film character. There always seems to be somebody who wants to kill him for some reason. Why doesn't he wear dark glasses? Then he wouldn't be recognised.

Joseph, son of Jacob – I   28
Biblical character, one of the 12 sons of Jacob. To show he was his favourite, his dad gave him a present – a coat of many colours.

Joseph, son of Jacob – II   68
Joseph's brothers, cheesed off because they

hadn't been given new coats, sold Joseph to some passing merchants. They explained Joseph's disappearance by telling Jacob that his favourite son had been eaten by a pack of wolves. Exhibit A: shredded coat of many colours.

Joseph, son of Jacob – III　　　　　111

Joseph ends up in Egypt and does pretty well, interpreting the Pharoah's dreams and saving them from famine. He is reunited with his daddy when the family come begging for food. It's a good story. Tim Rice and Andrew Lloyd Webber pinched it from the Bible.

Kent, Clark　　　　　78

Mild-mannered reporter, who was Superman underneath.

Kirk, Captain James T.　　　　　18

T.V. Commander of the Starship *Enterprise* which regularly boldly went where no man had gone before. And when he got there you could usually see why.

Lisa, Mona　　　　　44

Gently smiling subject of the most famous painting in the world.

Michaelangelo 16

Italian painter who spent a lot of time on his back. This was because he enjoyed painting on ceilings, the most famous of which is in the Sistine Chapel in Rome.

Moses 51

Biblical character, who led the escape of the Israelites from Egypt. Hotly pursued by the Pharoah's soldiers, the Israelites crossed the Red Sea when Moses parted the waters. The Egyptians weren't so lucky, and got drowned.

Nightingale, Florence 22

Nursing pioneer, fondly known as 'The Lady With That Blasted Lamp' by the patients she kept waking up to see if they were asleep.

Popeye 104

Cartoon character who gains strengh through stuffing spinach. This strength is usually employed in saving his skinny girlfriend, Olive Oyl, from the clutches of a great bruiser named Bluto.

Pythagoras 108

Greek mathematician, whose claim to everlasting fame lies in the theorem he discovered: 'the square on the hypotenuse of a right-angled triangle is equal to the sum of the squares on the other two sides.'

Quasimodo 69

Handicapped hero of Victor Hugo's book, 'The Hunchback of Notre Dame.' Saved the heroine from execution by swinging from the Notre Dame Cathedral's belfry by rope to haul her to safety.

Race, Roy 54

Comic-strip footballing hero, known as 'Roy of the Rovers' after the name of his team, Melchester Rovers. On a bad day he only scores a hat-trick.

Raleigh, Walter 71

Crawling English nobleman, said to have laid his cloak over a puddle so that Elizabeth the First didn't have to get her feet wet.

Samson 85

Biblical strong-man, whose strength disappeared when his hair was cut off while he was asleep.

Scrooge, Ebenezer 33

Main character in Charles Dicken's book, 'A Christmas Carol'. Hated Christmas.

Shakespeare, William   62

Greatest writer in the English language, which is why every pupil in the universe has to study the plays what he writ.

Tarzan   65

Fictional character brought up in the jungle by a bunch of apes. Spoke fluent ape, elephant, crocodile, but wasn't very good at English, French etc.

Tell, William   90

Legendary crossbow champion of Switzerland. His party trick was to shoot an apple off his son's head.

Terrestrial, Extra (E.T.)   26

Wrinkly little film star alien who got stuck on earth when he/she/it missed the last spaceship home and had to wait for the next one to come along.

Turpin, Richard (Dick)   14

Infamous highwayman whose catch-phrase was, 'Stand and deliver, your money or your life!' He must have been pretty strong – after all, he was always holding up stagecoaches. His career ended with a short period of suspension. He got hung.

Tutankhamun 24

Boy king of Egypt, c1360-1350 BC. Found in 1922, in a gold coffin. He was dead.

Vader, Darth 29

Nasty piece of work, featured in the film 'Star Wars'. Had a light-beam sword which he used to reduce the number of people in the cast.

Van Gogh, Vincent 12

Famous painter who went quite mad and cut off his own ear. There is no truth in the rumour that he carried out this dreadful act with the words, 'Ear today, gone tomorrow.'

White, Snow 73

Fairy story character who lived with seven dwarfs and fell into a deep sleep after eating a poisoned apple.

Who, Dr. 86

TV character who's brainy enough to travel through time and space, but not to get himself a sensible name.